trace & write
CURSIVE WRITING
Joining Letters

Published by

MAPLE PRESS PRIVATE LIMITED

Corporate & Editorial Office
A 63, Sector 58, Noida 201 301, U.P., India

phone: +91 120 455 3581, 455 3583
email: info@maplepress.co.in, website: www.maplepress.co.in

Printed in 2023 at Rashtriya Printers, Delhi, India

ISBN: 978-93-50334-89-8

10 9 8 7 6 5 4 3

Joining Letters A – Z

Trace the letters with a pencil. Then practice writing the letters on the lines.

aa   bb   cc   dd

Joining Letters A – Z

Trace the letters with a pencil. Then practice writing the letters on the lines.

ee   *ff*   *gg*   *hh*

Joining Letters A – Z

Trace the letters with a pencil. Then practice writing the letters on the lines.

ii   *jj*   *kk*   *ll*

Joining Letters A – Z

Trace the letters with a pencil. Then practice writing the letters on the lines.

mm   nn   oo   pp

Joining Letters A – Z

Trace the letters with a pencil. Then practice writing the letters on the lines.

qq *rr* *ss* *tt*

Joining Letters A – Z

Trace the letters with a pencil. Then practice writing the letters on the lines.

uuu   *vv*   *ww*   *xxx*

Joining Letters A – Z

Trace the letters with a pencil. Then practice writing the letters on the lines.

Joining Letters A – Z

Trace the letters with a pencil. Then practice writing the letters on the lines.

an at ac ad ab

an at ac ad ab

an at ac ad ab

an at ac ad ab

Joining Letters A – Z

Trace the letters with a pencil. Then practice writing the letters on the lines.

ba   *bc*   *bb*   *bd*

ba   *bc*   *bb*   *bd*

ba   *bc*   *bb*   *bd*

ba   *bc*   *bb*   *bd*

Joining Letters A – Z

Trace the letters with a pencil. Then practice writing the letters on the lines.

ca   cm   cg   ch

ca   cm   cg   ch

ca   cm   cg   ch

ca   cm   cg   ch

Joining Letters A – Z

Trace the letters with a pencil. Then practice writing the letters on the lines.

df   dv   dk   dl

df   dv   dk   dl

df   dv   dk   dl

df   dv   dk   dl

Joining Letters A – Z

Trace the letters with a pencil. Then practice writing the letters on the lines.

ea   *ec*   *em*   *ez*

Trace the letters with a pencil. Then practice writing the letters on the lines.

fc   fa   fk   fp

fc   fa   fk   fp

fc   fa   fk   fp

fc   fa   fk   fp

Joining Letters A – Z

Trace the letters with a pencil. Then practice writing the letters on the lines.

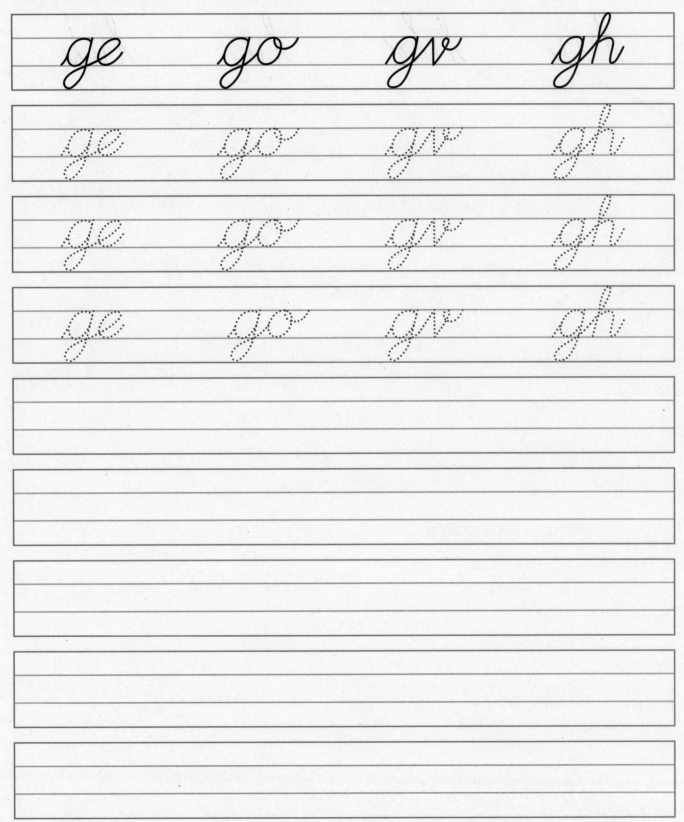

Joining Letters A – Z

Trace the letters with a pencil. Then practice writing the letters on the lines.

ha   hb   hc   hd

ha   hb   hc   hd

ha   hb   hc   hd

ha   hb   hc   hd

Joining Letters A – Z

Trace the letters with a pencil. Then practice writing the letters on the lines.

it　*in*　*ig*　*ip*

Joining Letters A – Z

Trace the letters with a pencil. Then practice writing the letters on the lines.

jc   jn   jo   jt

Joining Letters A – Z

Trace the letters with a pencil. Then practice writing the letters on the lines.

kc   km   kq   kr

kc   km   kq   kr

kc   km   kq   kr

kc   km   kq   kr

Joining Letters A – Z

Trace the letters with a pencil. Then practice writing the letters on the lines.

lm *lg* *lz* *lc*

Joining Letters A – Z

Trace the letters with a pencil. Then practice writing the letters on the lines.

ma   *mc*   *mp*   *mn*

ma   *mc*   *mp*   *mn*

ma   *mc*   *mp*   *mn*

ma   *mc*   *mp*   *mn*

Joining Letters A – Z

Trace the letters with a pencil. Then practice writing the letters on the lines.

na   *ng*   *ng*   *nd*

Joining Letters A – Z

Trace the letters with a pencil. Then practice writing the letters on the lines.

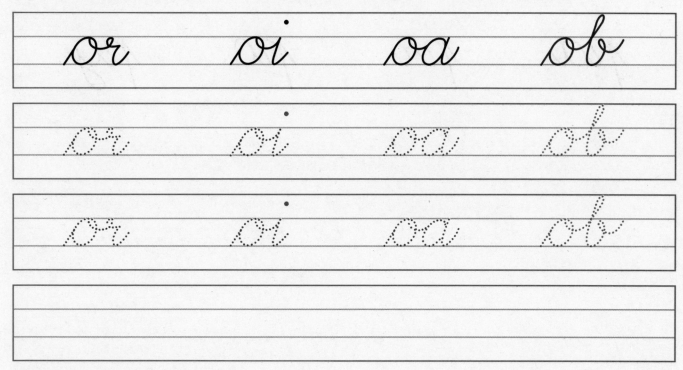

Joining Letters A – Z

Trace the letters with a pencil. Then practice writing the letters on the lines.

Joining Letters A – Z

Trace the letters with a pencil. Then practice writing the letters on the lines.

pa   pr   pc   pg

pa   pr   pc   pg

pa   pr   pc   pg

pa   pr   pc   pg

Joining Letters A – Z

Trace the letters with a pencil. Then practice writing the letters on the lines.

rd	*rc*	*rn*	*rg*

rd   *rc*   *rn*   *rg*

rd   *rc*   *rn*   *rg*

rd   *rc*   *rn*   *rg*

Joining Letters A – Z

Trace the letters with a pencil. Then practice writing the letters on the lines.

sg   sn   so   sf

Joining Letters A – Z

Trace the letters with a pencil. Then practice writing the letters on the lines.

to   tn   td   tf

to   tn   td   tf

to   tn   td   tf

to   tn   td   tf

Joining Letters A – Z

Trace the letters with a pencil. Then practice writing the letters on the lines.

uo   *ur*

Joining Letters A – Z

Trace the letters with a pencil. Then practice writing the letters on the lines.

Nr   *Ni*   *Ng*   *No*

Joining Letters A – Z

Trace the letters with a pencil. Then practice writing the letters on the lines.

wc   we   wi   wr

Joining Letters A – Z

Trace the letters with a pencil. Then practice writing the letters on the lines.

xa   *xb*   *xc*   *xd*

Joining Letters A – Z

Trace the letters with a pencil. Then practice writing the letters on the lines.

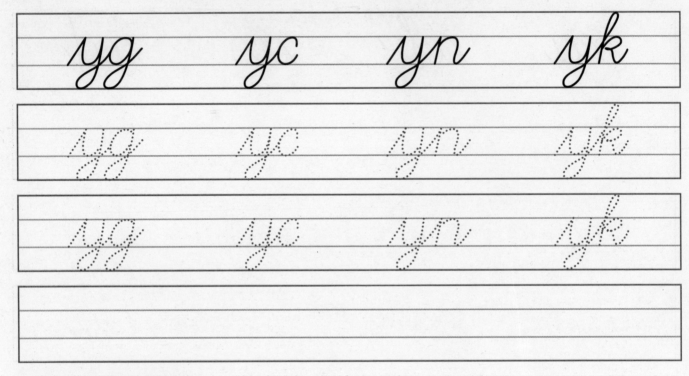

Joining Letters A – Z

Trace the letters with a pencil. Then practice writing the letters on the lines.